MW00449405

Vision Mapping™ Workbook

Introducing the "Idea Realization Continuum™"

by James S. Gordon

Copyright James S. Gordon, 2002-2017

Acknowledgments

Amazon.com has made it very easy for me to author ebooks and books in print. I am very grateful for this platform wherein I have been able to publish my first two books – this is the third.

I have two additional books planned for 2017. Both volumes are from another author – a family member. Thanks, Amazon.com

Speaking of family members, I have a first cousin and a third cousin who have books for sale on Amazon.com. What is strange about this fact is that I have never met these two cousins. I found out about their work from her dad (first cousin) and her grandmother (third cousin), respectively. We all have different genres…Thanks, Amazon.com

I trust that if you have a book project in you that you will not postpone getting started with it. This book can be a way to begin putting legs under your book or other project that you have – that project which is trying to manifest itself through you.

Let's get started, now!

Introduction

My first book was "How to Succeed at Personal Planning and Goal Setting Workbook". It covered goal discovery and goal "distillation" – helping the user to create a plan that she or he could work. That was a "bottom up planning process". And I found that many of the students that I shared this system with were able to complete the planning and goal setting tools with relative ease.

The chief difference between the Goal Discovery... and "Vision Mapping™" is that Vision mapping™ is a top-down planning system that is scalable to the limits of one's imagination. It can be used at home or in a Fortune 100 company.

A basic premise of Vision Mapping™ is that it employs the **track ideas run on towards completion"** . In fact, I'll extend that sentiment to say Vision Mapping™ **maps your route to the results that you seek.**

Vision Mapping™ is the product of 30+ years of professional experience - experience which includes developing and conducting training events in Human Resources, Economic and Workforce Development, Financial Planning, Personal Development and Entrepreneur Success Training.

At its simplest, Vision Mapping™ is comprised of a model representing the continuum that ideas traverse towards their fulfillment, a model for the aggregation of Vision MAPs™, and a model for aligning the Vision MAPs™ of multiple individuals, multiple departments or divisions of an organization.

Vision Mapping™ is to personal and strategic planning what Global Positioning Systems (GPS) are to Geography as the Vision Continuum™ and Vision MAPs™ provide each user with immediate and precise feedback. This feedback "**localizes**" or pinpoints the user's position in relation to the end result that the user is working towards.

No longer do we (or our loved ones) need to meander through life - uncertain as to the steps needed to reach our goals. Vision Mapping™ helps us to **start right, stay right and end right** when setting and accomplishing Goals!

NOTE: I have added <u>older graphics</u> that I used in my Vision Mapping™ workshops (sorry that they are not high quality). And, I have added a few blank graphics, too, for your use in this workbook.

Table of Contents

Chapter 1 – The Vision Continuum™ aka The Idea Realization Continuum™

We are beginning the process of creating the inputs for your first Vision MAP™. It starts with a list (or a single item if you wish) of the desired outcome(s) that you'd like to accomplish first or next. However, before that we must start out using the same language, i.e. agree to the meaning of the terms we will be using.

The Vision Continuum™ is "the track that ideas run on towards completion" - it **"maps your route to the results that you seek".** The resulting Vision MAP™:

- Encompasses the idea-to-realization continuum or pathway.

- Is created from building blocks. Each section of the **Vision MAP™** is built out from the preceding Vision Continuum™ component.

- Each section is an area of (in) development.

- Illustrates planning and goal-setting with the end result in mind and on paper or computer.

Reference Book Definitions

Please indulge me by going online and/or to your nearest reference books and looking up the definitions for the following five terms. If you write down the definitions you will be able to refer back to them, shortly. Thanks!

If you would like to challenge yourself, please start by writing your own definitions to the five terms, below. Then compare your responses to those in your reference materials.

Reference Source #1:

1. Vision:

2. Mission

3. Plan:

4. Goal:

5. Objective:

Reference Source #2:

1. Vision:

2. Mission

3. Plan:

4. Goal:

5. Objective:

Reference Source #3:

1. Vision:

2. Mission

3. Plan:

4. Goal:

5. Objective:

Reference Source #4:

1. Vision:

2. Mission

3. Plan:

4. Goal:

5. Objective:

Reference Source #5:

1. Vision:

2. Mission

3. Plan:

4. Goal:

5. Objective:

Idea Realization Continuum™

The Vision Continuum™ (Idea Realization Continuum™) is the path on which visions (ideas) progress towards realization. Think of it as "**your route to the results that you seek**".

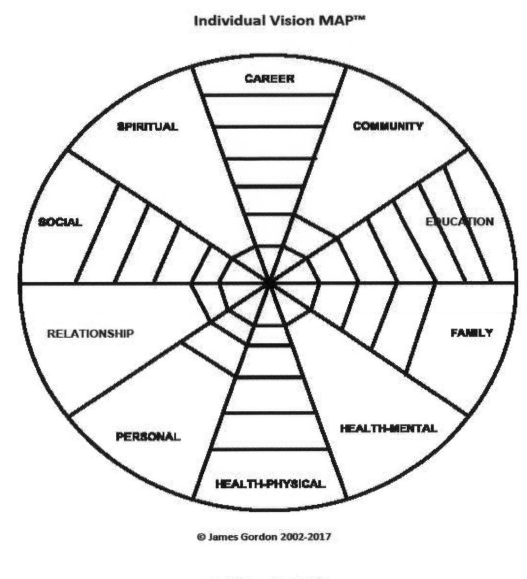

Individual Vision MAP™

© James Gordon 2002-2017

Copyright - James S. Gordon 2002

NOTE: I have added <u>older graphics</u> that I used in my Vision Mapping™ workshops (sorry that they are not of higher quality). And, I have added a blank graphic (below), too, for your use in this workbook.

Individual Vision MAP™

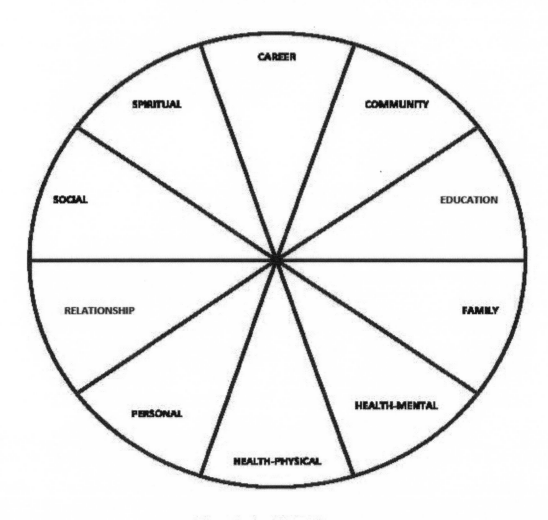

©James Gordon 2002-2017

The vertical lines within the triangle are drawn when that step is completed.

Essentially each Vision MAP™ begins with a list of your desired or needed outcome(s)

in each area of your personal life that you wish to address. Then we add the vision for each desired or needed outcome per the definitions of these terms, below. Next, we write out each of the succeeding components as outlined in our illustrations and glossary. When these components of the Vision MAP™ are aggregated one can immediately see what step(s) has been done and what steps have yet to be done. More on this, shortly.

- How close did your definitions compare with those of the reference materials that you consulted?

- In what respects were your definitions different from your selected reference definitions?

- Were your reference materials helpful to you in terms of giving you a clear understanding for each term? If not, why not?

- To what extent were the reference materials the same?

- …different from one another?

- Are you now more or less clear as to the "standard" definitions of each of the five terms?

I'll share the results of my "research" next. Part of that research is in Appendix B.

Definitions for the Idea Realization Continuum™ Components:

1. <u>VISION</u> is a strong emotion or feelings-based Purpose **PLUS** a Picture(s) of the Desired or Required Outcome. Vision can be experienced as an idea or feeling regarding the desired outcome, which is held in mind and/or heart. **Keywords:** ***Seeing and/or Feeling the Desired Outcome as accomplished***.

2. <u>MISSION</u> is the objectification or out-picturing of a Vision. Clothing of the vision begins here. A Mission is the **direction to** or the **direction from** some thing or someone - based on one's present position. **Thinking, Feeling, & Behaviors** are channeled in a given direction(s). **Keywords:** ***Direction to or Direction from***.

3. <u>PLAN</u> is a **written** statement of Goals, Objectives, Tasks & Resources + Options (Plan B, C, etc.) A plan answers the 5 Ws of journalism…who, what, why, where, when and how - and it includes a SWOT (Strengths, Weaknesses, Opportunities, and Threats) Analysis or What if scenarios. **Keyword*: Assessment.***

4. <u>GOAL</u> is a thing to be obtained, given, shared, done or a state of being to be attained. During this step, Timetables & Milestones (Metrics) are developed. **Keywords:** ***Metrics established and/or communicated.***

5. OBJECTIVE is a step(s) to be taken to achieve or attain a goal. **Keywords: _Stepping Stones to Goals._**

6. TASK is an activity that cannot be sub-divided any further in the attainment of an objective. To Do Items are typically Tasks. **Keywords: _A Discreet Action._**

7. END RESULT = the cumulative effect of the foregoing series of activities.

Part of my motivation for consulting more than a dozen reference volumes is that I found no clear or "universal" meanings for our terms. Sometimes, one term was used to define another term. So, I ended up being more confused after this research than before…

My need for the information stemmed from the Life Skills training that I developed and conducted for local social service agencies. It was necessary for me to get everyone on the same page as we examined the ends and outs of goal setting and planning for each of the 3,000 or so people who attended that training.

Here are just a few more terms that I will define for our use:

DESIRED OUTCOME = Enriched Vision = The result planned for, hoped for, and towards which **effort and resources** are directed.

STRATEGY = exercising and/or communicating forethought regarding the linking of each successive element of the Vision Continuum™ or Idea Realization Continuum™ [iterations of a vision] through to its end result. **MACRO or inter-Vision Continua™**

TACTIC = exercising and/or communicating forethought regarding the execution of an element within a Vision Continuum™ component. **MICRO or intra-Vision Continuum™**

The seven numbered terms above form the basic glossary / lexicon for the Vision Mapping™ system. These terms can easily be taught (scaled) to K-6 students and these definitions will serve our youth a lifetime as they become successful Vision Mappers™ – Vision Cartographers™ in their own right.

The Vision MAP™ is an aggregation of Vision Continua™, which are assembled for a specific (planning) purpose, e.g. education, vacation, optimal health, an individual / team / organizational result.

Vision Continuum - tm
Horizontal View

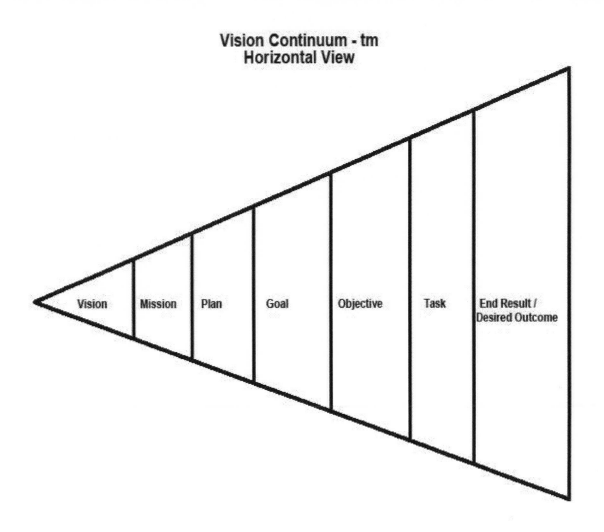

Vision | Mission | Plan | Goal | Objective | Task | End Result / Desired Outcome

Copyright - James S. Gordon 2002

19

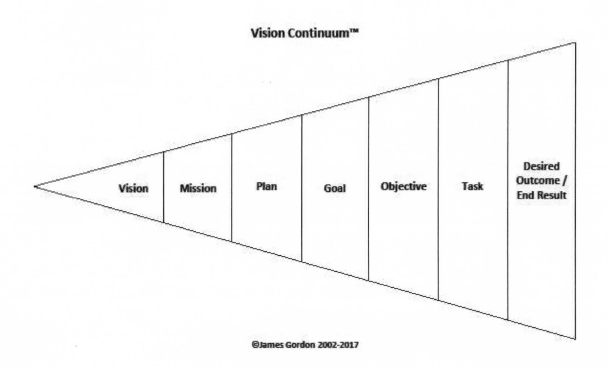

Vision Continuum™

Vision | Mission | Plan | Goal | Objective | Task | Desired Outcome / End Result

©James Gordon 2002-2017

20

Vision MAPs™ are to be aggregated from (individual Vision Continuums™) and those Vision MAPs™ are then aligned based on user selected criteria, e.g. keyword(s), chronology, or other metric(s).

Each person's Vision MAP™ will likely be as distinct as her or his fingerprint. This is due, in part, to the fact that goals and objectives typically differ from one individual to the next. But even if two people had the same goals and objectives – it is highly unlikely that they are also at the same stage of development for those respective goals and objectives and less likely still that they will envision identical futures.

Chapter 2 – Introduction to Vision MAPping™

Our Current State

Imagine watching a play or movie and people are dressed up in a horse's costume - level 1's vision is the head, levels 2-5 represent the body and level 6 is the "rear". In an organization, the level below has a different "world view" than the level above. This can lead to conflict over visions and missions or goals and objectives and what comes first or next, etc. That is part of the reason that we started with definitions of the terms that are – in play – to come to an agreement as to the meaning of the terms in our "glossary".

Here is an illustration of that phenomenon:

Tiered Vision MAP™

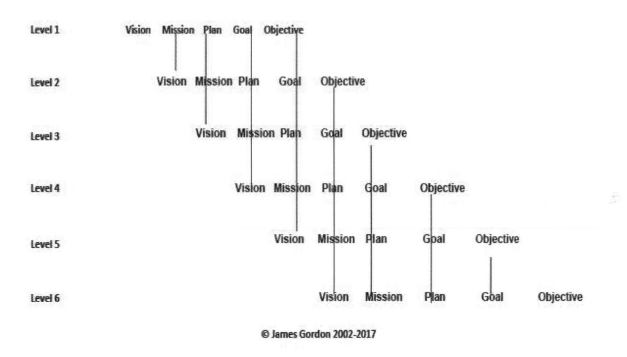

© James Gordon 2002-2017

Copyright - James S. Gordon 2002

As we examine the Tiered Vision MAP™ more closely, we see that the Mission of Level 1 becomes the Vision of Level 2; the Mission of Level 2 becomes the Vision of Level 3 and so on it goes for each successive level. The Goal and Objective of one level is similarly transferred to the level below it (in a staggered pattern) – down to the lowest

23

levels of the organization. Hence, one group will refer to their vision when speaking with someone on a lower level who sees a mission instead of a vision – this also applies to goals and objectives which are being discussed in "mixed company" – so to speak.

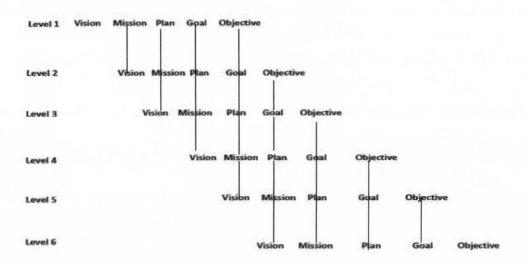

Tiered Vision MAP™

©James Gordon 2002-2017

Chapter 3 - Vision MAP™ Components

First, let's make a list of the key areas of your life that you have set goals for or want to set goals in. There is no right number or right answer for the number of key areas one must or should have. My example uses ten. If you have twenty, simply place ten in each circle. That way, you'd be able to examine them, side-by-side.

With this display, one can easily see the / an author's self-assessment regarding her progress in each of the ten areas displayed.

The completed stages are represented by the vertical lines of the Vision Continuum™. The lines are only added **after** a step has been completed. If there is a need to display the entire Vision MAP™ prior to its completion, the author could use broken or "wavy" lines to indicate that that step is not yet complete.

Let's see what we can glean from the example of Jill – a hypothetical end user. It looks like she is in the process of planning the health and fitness component of her Vision

MAP™ while she is achieving the desired outcome (aka end result) in terms of completing her Ph.D. as part of the education component to her Vision MAP™.

Jill can see that other areas of her Vision MAP™ could use the same quality and quantity of care that she applied to her health and education Vision Continua™. The other areas do not yet have the vertical lines telling her that part of her Vision MAP™ is awaiting her attention, at some point.

This level of detail helps us to "start right and stay right so that we can end right" as a successful Vision Mapper™. With each Vision Continuum™ that you add to your Vision MAP™, you gain **clarity** and **proximity to** the desired outcome that you seek.

Chapter 4 – Basic Types of Vision MAPs™

Individual Vision MAP™

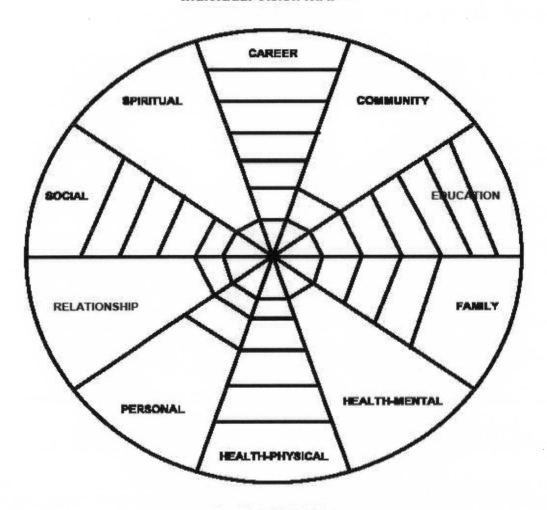

© James Gordon 2002-2017

Copyright - James S. Gordon 2002

Let's make some (more) assumptions about Jill - based on the Vision MAP™ displayed, above.

We might surmise that she is in her chosen career as her education Vision Continuum™ indicates (by way of the vertical line) that the end result or desired outcome has been attained. However, her spiritual vision and mental health vision are yet to be "fleshed out" or realized.

Adding that vertical line to the Vision Continuum™, in question, demonstrates to the "owner" of the Vision MAP™ that she is on track towards the accomplishment or attainment of the Vision stated in her Vision MAP™ (sometimes shortened to VMAP).

If Jill chose to share her VMAP with a close friend or relative, how much of a learning curve would be needed for that close friend or relative to understand what the VMAP is showing her or him? If you can answer that question, then you've already learned the basics for this Vision Mapping™ system.

I believe that Vision Mapping™ can be "scaled" to meet the needs of grade school children. First, with the simple terms it uses, then later with the worthwhile inclusion of school – then personal goals…

Individual Vision MAP™ Blank

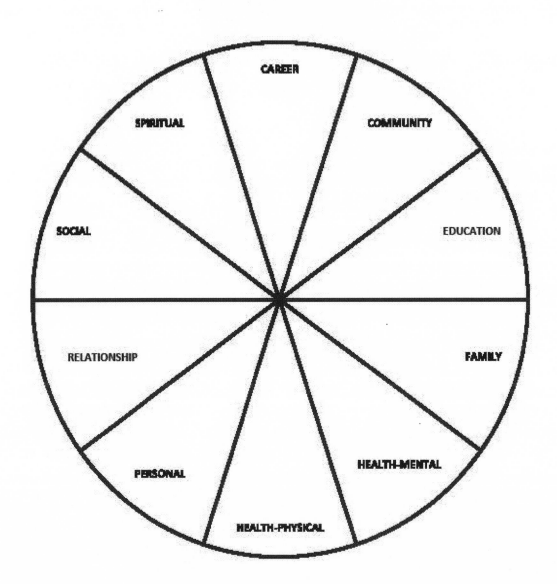

©James Gordon 2002-2017

Role Vision MAP™

Rather than preparing a list of criteria for your first Individual Vision MAP™, you may opt to list criteria for a Role Vision MAP™. Some of the "role" criteria, the owner selected were:

1. Mother/Father
2. Sister/Brother
3. Wife/Husband
4. Friend
5. Volunteer
6. Athlete
7. Entrepreneur
8. Employee

To this list, you may add any term that expresses who you see yourself as. Some of you (will) have the privilege of helping others to complete their own Vision MAPs™. Having both a robust and relevant list of input for each person – whether family member, friend, student, or co-worker is key to that person's success with this process.

Role Vision MAP™

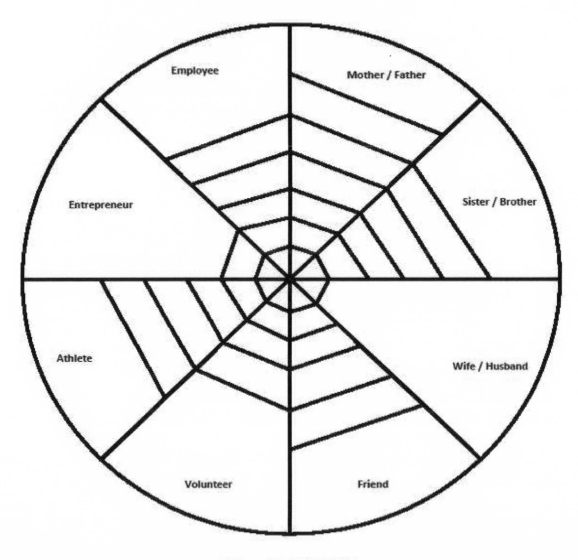

© James Gordon 2002-2017

Copyright - James S. Gordon 2002

Role Vision MAP™ Blank

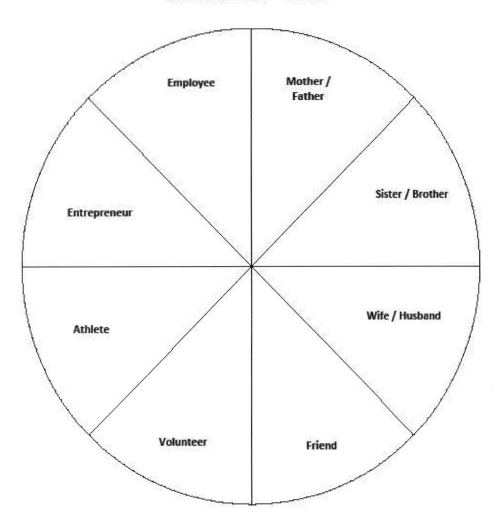

©James Gordon 2002-2017

In high school and college, I had the honor, privilege, and joy of being a team captain (track and cross country) for five of the seven years that I participated in those activities. For some of us, leading a team may happen with jobs we hold or businesses that we run. I trust that you have the opportunity to experience the positive attributes of a successful team.

It may be that your successful team experience is being a head of household. That experience, too, must be approached as an honor and privilege for those that lead on the home front – your best is also required there.

The team VMAP like the VMAPs before it contains the flexibility that you need to make it work for you – to change your specific inputs – to make your list(s) – to add to the VMAP as you see fit. Check your progress against the metrics that you have created using this system.

Team Vision MAP™

Raison d'etre roughly translates, from the French, as reason for being… Your Team Vision MAP™ will likely be different and dynamic – changing from time to time as your life and work situations dictate.

Unlike the Individual or Role VMAPs, the Team Vision MAP™ will require the input from all the members of that team who meet virtually or in person to decide what track(s) their collective visions run on.

I've included three variations of the way that these Team VMAPs are displayed - one will be circular, the second will be a table, and the third will be a grid – each containing identical information. However, you may also choose to use a list – as a fourth viable option.

The display method that you choose should be amenable to the team that will be using it. They should be able to update it or recommend other ways to make it more user friendly to other team members.

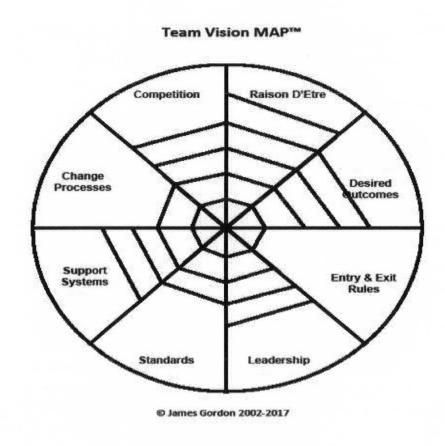

Team Vision MAP™

Competition

Raison D'Etre

Change Processes

Desired Outcomes

Support Systems

Entry & Exit Rules

Standards

Leadership

© James Gordon 2002-2017

Copyright - James S. Gordon 2002

Personally, I like the detail of the "grid", below. Any VMAP can give you a certain

degree of granularity not found in most planning and goal setting tools – I've looked…

Team Vision MAP™ - Grid

Vision M.A.P. Grid - tm
for Team Vision M.A.P. - tm

	Vision	Mission	Plan(s)	Goal(s)	Objective(s)	Task(s)	Desired Outcome
Reason for Being	1	1.1 1.2 1.3	1.1.1 1.1.2 1.1.3	1.1.1.1 1.1.1.2 1.1.1.3	1.1.1.1.1 1.1.1.1.2 1.1.1.1.3	1.1.1.1.1.1 1.1.1.1.1.2 1.1.1.1.1.3	
Results	2	2.1 2.2 2.3	2.1.1 2.1.2 2.1.3	2.1.1.1 2.1.1.2 2.1.1.3	2.1.1.1.1 2.1.1.1.2 2.1.1.1.3	2.1.1.1.1.1 2.1.1.1.1.2 2.1.1.1.1.3	
Entry & Exit Rules	3	3.1 3.2 3.3	3.1.1 3.1.2 3.1.3	3.1.1.1 3.1.1.2 3.1.1.3	3.1.1.1.1 3.1.1.1.2 3.1.1.1.3	3.1.1.1.1.1 3.1.1.1.1.2 3.1.1.1.1.3	
Leadership	4	4.1 4.2 4.3	4.1.1 4.1.2 4.1.3	4.1.1.1 4.1.1.2 4.1.1.3	4.1.1.1.1 4.1.1.1.2 4.1.1.1.3	4.1.1.1.1.1 4.1.1.1.1.2 4.1.1.1.1.3	
Standards	5	5.1 5.2 5.3	5.1.1 5.1.2 5.1.3	5.1.1.1 5.1.1.2 5.1.1.3	5.1.1.1.1 5.1.1.1.2 5.1.1.1.3	5.1.1.1.1.1 5.1.1.1.1.2 5.1.1.1.1.3	
Support Systems	6	6.1 6.2 6.3	6.1.1 6.1.2 6.1.3	6.1.1.1 6.1.1.2 6.1.1.3	6.1.1.1.1 6.1.1.1.2 6.1.1.1.3	6.1.1.1.1.1 6.1.1.1.1.2 6.1.1.1.1.3	
Change Processes	7	7.1 7.2 7.3	7.1.1 7.1.2 7.1.3	7.1.1.1 7.1.1.2 7.1.1.3	7.1.1.1.1 7.1.1.1.2 7.1.1.1.3	7.1.1.1.1.1 7.1.1.1.1.2 7.1.1.1.1.3	
Competition	8	8.1 8.2 8.3	8.1.1 8.1.2 8.1.3	8.1.1.1 8.1.1.2 8.1.1.3	8.1.1.1.1 8.1.1.1.2 8.1.1.1.3	8.1.1.1.1.1 8.1.1.1.1.2 8.1.1.1.1.3	

Copyright - James S. Gordon 2002

Team Vision MAP™ - Table

Team Vision MAP™ Table

	Vision	Mission	Plan(s)	Goal(s)	Objective(s)	Task(s)	Desired Outcome
Raison D'Etre							
Competition							
Entry & Exit Rules							
Leadership							
Standards							
Support Systems							
Change Processes							

© James Gordon 2002-2017

Copyright - James S. Gordon 2002

Organization Vision MAP™

The next Vision MAP™ is for an organization (of any kind) that you affiliate with. Our focus here will be your job or business. Again, the items for you may differ – widely – that's okay.

Your place of business, worship, volunteerism, and/or leisure are all candidates for your Vision MAPping™ activities. With these tools, you will increase your own as well as others' understanding of the work and direction of the organization – for its collective benefit.

Areas of opportunity / growth become visually apparent - quickly as we engage in this process of Vision MAPping™ what's important to us.

The Vision MAP™ below is a guide as to form not content. I've used Microsoft's Visio for these older drawings along with a Smart Draw product – for true amateurs or novices – which describes my artistic talent…

I have developed and conducted supervisory, management, and entrepreneurial trainings for a variety of organizations. The areas of training that I enjoyed most (second only to life skills training) were the strategic planning / strategic management activities. The following VMAP outlines common organizational foci for operating the business / organization.

As before, we start by listing the essential areas wherein feedback is required to run the business or agency, in question. Again, if you have more responsibilities in your organization, business, or agency, add a second VMAP or a third, if needed.

What we are doing is taking a **snapshot** of the organization, team, or individual. And future snapshots can be scheduled at regular intervals to measure the progress that the organization makes.

Organization Vision MAP™

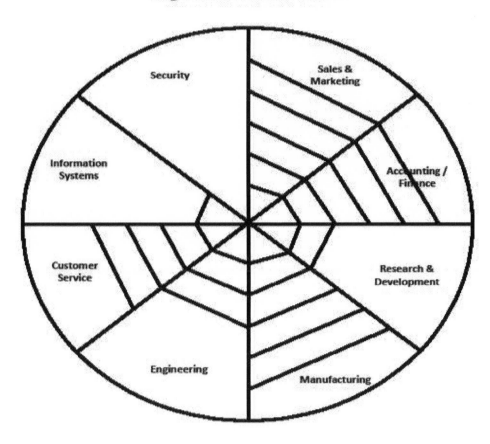

© James Gordon 2002-2017

Copyright – James S. Gordon 2002

41

Competitive Advantage

Vision Mapping™ includes a template for corporate Vision MAPs™. As a bonus feature, it also includes a means of assessing an organization's strategic management posture. In the absence of a "working" model, these tools can help an organization to better identify and meet the needs of its customers by better identifying its own:

- **Market Posture**

- **Value Creation Posture**

- **Competencies Posture**

- **Resources Commitment Posture**

Armed with these tools, an organization can more confidently and effectively acquire, secure and increase its market share.

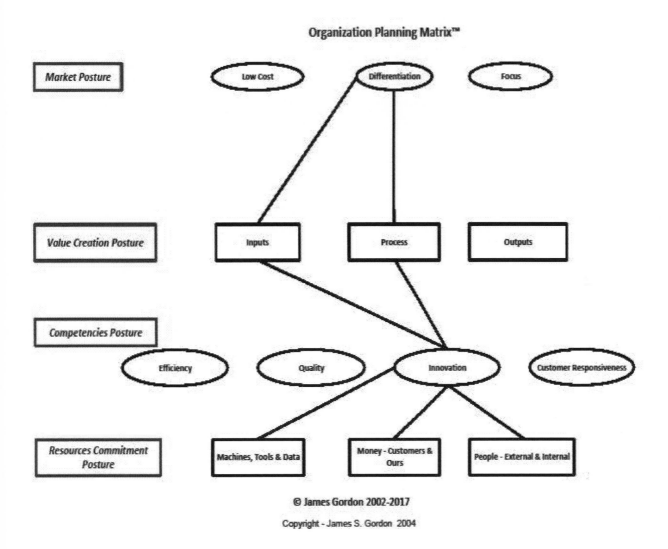

Organization Planning Matrix™

Market Posture — Low Cost · Differentiation · Focus

Value Creation Posture — Inputs · Process · Outputs

Competencies Posture — Efficiency · Quality · Innovation · Customer Responsiveness

Resources Commitment Posture — Machines, Tools & Data · Money - Customers & Ours · People - External & Internal

© James Gordon 2002-2017

Copyright - James S. Gordon 2004

This graphic planning matrix was adapted from information in the textbook, "Strategic Management" by Drs. Charles Hill and Gareth Jones.

The lines connecting the components of this VMAP represent a snapshot of my business – circa 2004. Your business may have a "Market Posture" that blends a low-cost posture

43

plus a focus posture, e.g. with a Medicare supplement insurance product that is meant to be tailored to those that are eligible for Medicare and who are interested in saving money on that product.

This is the behind-the-scenes look at the same VMAP. Each relevant part to the company performing the analyses is illustrated, below. On the surface, we have what seems like a bunch of pinwheels – streamed together. But, each VMAP contains a tremendous amount of "shorthand" as to the current state and direction for the organization and each individual within that organization – including its teams, departments, divisions or other groups that comprise the organization.

Corporate Planning Matrix - tm

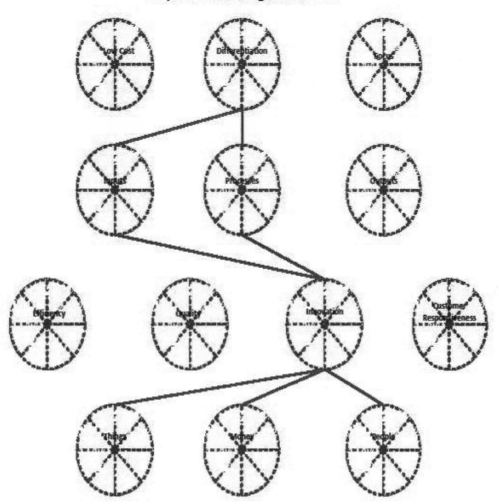

Copyright - James S. Gordon 2002

45

Chapter 5 - What is Vision MAP Alignment™ ?

- A springboard to the alignment of multiple visions.
- A snapshot of understanding.
- A benchmark for further development / research.

An alignment of VMAPs is simply means to aggregate logical combinations of VMAPs, e.g. individual-team-department or company. Or, it could means aggregating an individual VMAP with one for marriage and family.

Meta Vision MAP Alignment™

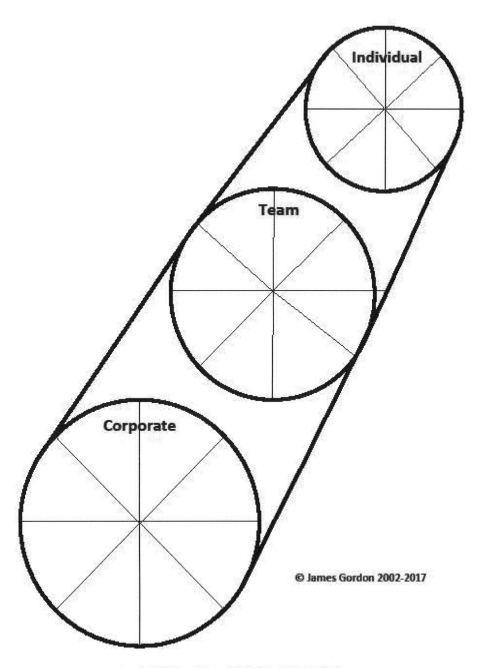

Individual

Team

Corporate

© James Gordon 2002-2017

Copyright - James S. Gordon 2002

As a business owner, one could have 200 employees in a dozen teams. Each employee as well as each team could have its own VMAP - with its respective visions, missions, plans, etc. – can all be aligned using this tool.

The Meta Vision MAP™ extends the boundary of the VMAP to a larger population – more scenarios. Meta Vision MAPs™ combine multiple people, ideas, and / or items into a new "arrangement" or alignment.

Meta Vision MAP™

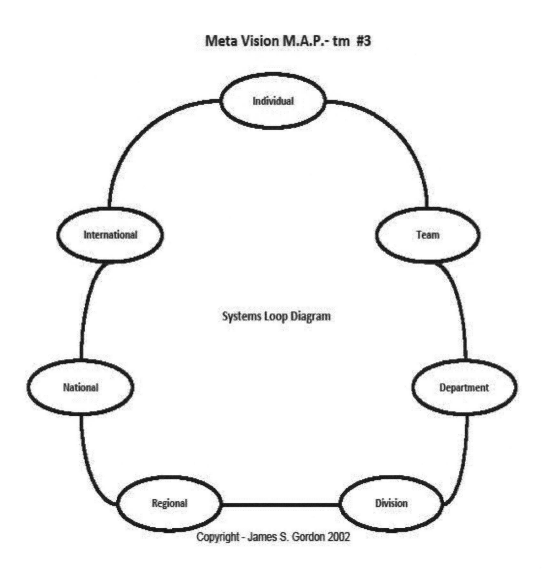

Meta Vision M.A.P.- tm #3

Individual

International

Team

Systems Loop Diagram

National

Department

Regional

Division

Copyright - James S. Gordon 2002

The behind-the-scenes look at this diagram yields the following:

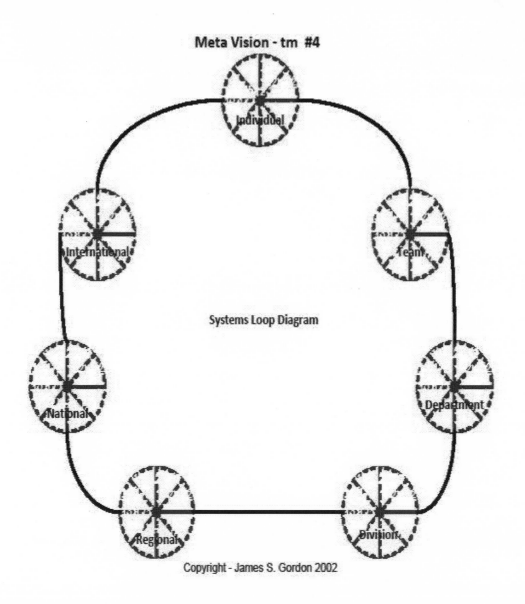

Meta Vision - tm #4

Systems Loop Diagram

Copyright - James S. Gordon 2002

The individual VMAP is subsumed by the team VMAP – then by each respective level of the organization, in question. One finds these VMAPs "nested" in the next level of the organization, as above.

Let's back off from "organization" VMAPs and get more personal about our VMAPping.

Marriage Vision MAP™

So far, you've created your first Individual Vision MAP™. Let's quickly look at two other components of a family VMAP "package", if you will. First, the Marriage Vision MAP™ and then the Family Vision MAP™.

There will be overlap in Vision MAPs™. Recall that we briefly looked at a Role VMAP, above. With different roles, you may find some similar and some competing interests – that's to be expected.

Marriage Vision MAP™

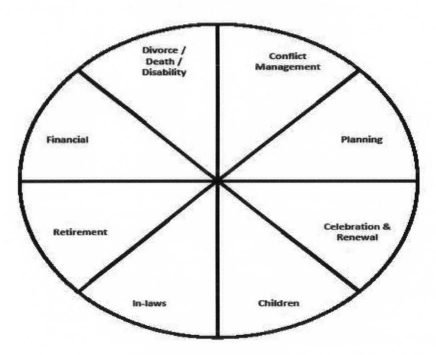

© James Gordon 2002-2017

Copyright - James S. Gordon 2002

Family Vision MAP™

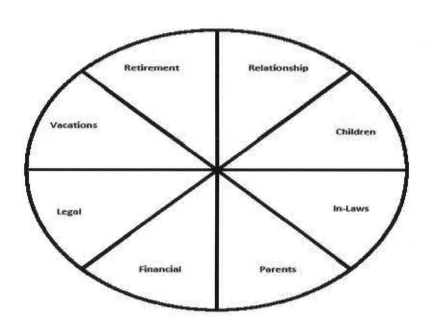

Family Vision M.A.P. - tm

Copyright - James S. Gordon 2002

Until we develop some fancy modeling software for VMAPs, printing them and viewing them side-by-side, this VMAP will help you assess the need for alignment or re-alignment at home or at work.

Family Vision MAP™

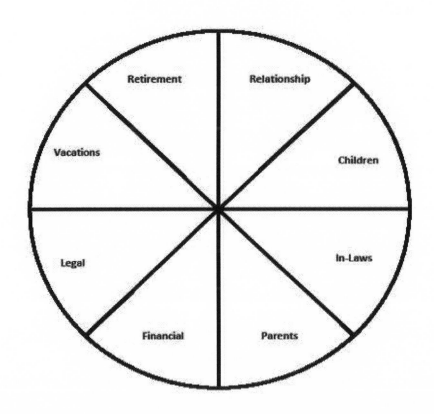

© James Gordon 2002-2017

Copyright - James S. Gordon 2002

Family Vision MAP Alignment™

As the head of household, your interest in Vision Mapping™ may simply be to help you and your family attain the growth, development and adjustment goals needed for each family member's well-being.

Meta Vision MAP Alignment™

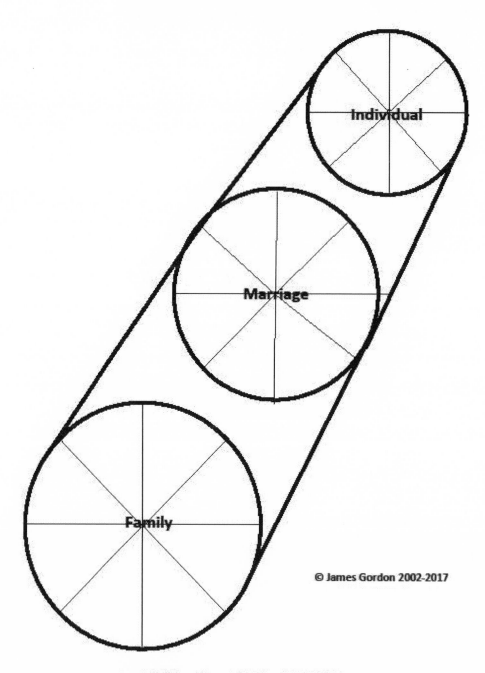

Individual

Marriage

Family

© James Gordon 2002-2017

Copyright - James S. Gordon 2002

One might ask, does one start with the family or organization VMAP Alignment? What are your priorities? In my first book, "How to Succeed at Personal Planning and Goal Setting Workbook", I included a tool called "Goal Circles", which helps an individual begin the process of comparing and contrasting "competing" goals and sorting priorities for the parties involved…

With Vision MAPping™, partners can review and reconcile one another's VMAPs – resolve conflict and align the VMAPs.

Chapter 6 – The Vision Breakdown Structure™

The simple Vision Continuum™ diagram in the first chapters can be "morphed" into a more complex (looking) Vision Breakdown Structure™. The Vision Breakdown Structure™ serves as **your route to the results** that you seek. As a forensic tool the Vision Breakdown Structure™ allows the user to re-trace her path to success or failure. The Vision Breakdown Structure™ also serves as a forecasting tool, again - **your route to the results** that you seek.

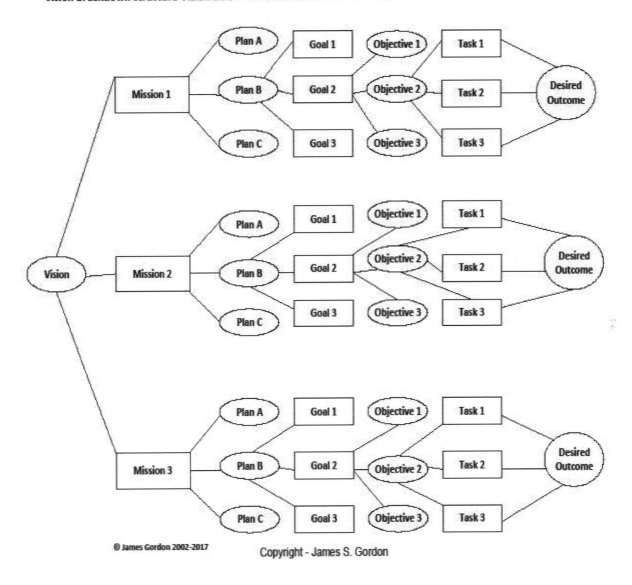

© James Gordon 2002-2017   Copyright - James S. Gordon

I used the Vision Breakdown Structure™, above, to map out my plan for optimal health.

Briefly, Mission 1 was to manage food (intake) and supplementation, Mission 2 was to

ensure that I continued my exercise routine, and Mission 3 was to ensure spiritual

pursuits that lead to and sustain harmony --- equanimity.

Chapter 7 - Education and Vision Mapping™

The first (of three) examples for the application of the Vision Mapping™ system will be in the field of Education. The benefits of Vision Mapping™ for students, their parents, teachers, and staff can be summed up by way of the following analogy:

Having a Global Positioning System (GPS) in your vehicle gives you an added since of confidence and security in terms of reaching the destination that **you** have chosen. Vision MAPping™ is just as **precise** in terms of locating your position and your destination on your **Route to Results™** and **you** will feel just as **confident** and **secure** in terms of reaching **your** destination, i.e. your desired or required outcome.

Vision Mapping™ for / in Education - Our common interest is in exploring and developing answers to the question "How do we best serve the students in our schools? Part of that answer is in bringing together the best teachers, the best staff and the best contractors and vendors – who share this common desire – serving our students.

Invennovate, LLC is a company, which values life-long learning. Planning is an activity which will serve us for our entire lives. On a daily basis, we will engage in planning and successfully executing those plans - with varying degrees of success in terms of realizing our desired outcomes.

The first point to mention when examining the School District Vision MAP™ is that the respective categories will differ from one district to the next. However, there may be a core set of categories that are the same among most or all school districts. The ones that we chose are for illustration purposes only.

Parental Perspective - In this example, our hypothetical set of parents visit the school district to discuss options for their 2 year old. During the discussion, our hypothetical administrator pulls out the following diagram and discusses educational transitions for the child. The diagram is what we see, below.

The transitions which are listed on this VMAP are:

- Home to Pre-school
- Pre-school to Kindergarten
- Kindergarten to Elementary
- Elementary to Middle School
- Middle to High School
- High School to College
- College to Career

This VMAP is a detailed depiction of Educational Transitions the child will encounter during her education. Each area of transition contains one (or more) Vision, Mission, etc. This type of Vision MAP™ is entitled a Meta Vision MAP™ as it encompasses the macro view of an area under consideration – educational transitions.

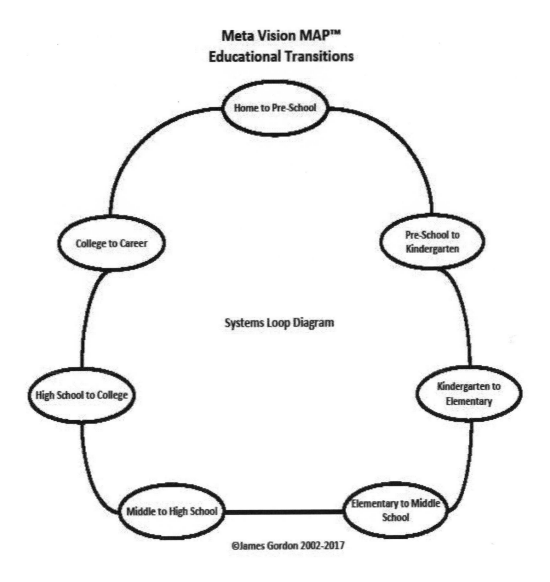

Meta Vision MAP™
Educational Transitions

Home to Pre-School

College to Career

Pre-School to Kindergarten

Systems Loop Diagram

High School to College

Kindergarten to Elementary

Middle to High School

Elementary to Middle School

©James Gordon 2002-2017

Each of the oval components of this Vision MAP™ is comprised of a Vision

Continuum™ (triangle shaped graphic above) – featuring the Vision through Desired

Outcome steps that we've been discussing.

Next the administrator shows the parents two Vision MAPs™ taken from the work of

Erik Erikson. The first Vision MAP™ pertains to the "Healthy Development Stages" of

an individual.

Erik Erikson's Healthy Development Stages Vision MAP

The second Vision MAP™ details the "Unhealthy Development Stages". The purpose of this discussion is to help the young parents understand that they play a vital role in the healthy preparation of their child for school as well as for positive citizenship as their child matures.

Erik Erikson's Unhealthy
Development Stages Vision
MAP

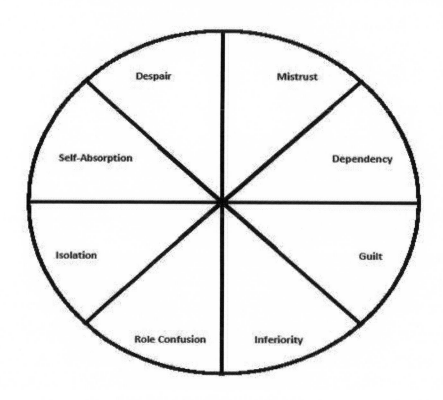

Student Vision MAP™ - The third perspective is that of the student. The Student Vision MAP™ contains the following hypothetical subjects for that student's typical day. Each subject (or period) during the day offers the student an opportunity to progress towards her or his vision of the value or purpose of the subject in terms of how it contributes to the student's life, well-being, or career.

If your child's day is comprised of more or fewer periods – please add or trim them from the VMAP shown. If she has no job, there is still an opportunity to discuss what the world of work expects from a "newcomer".

Student Vision MAP™

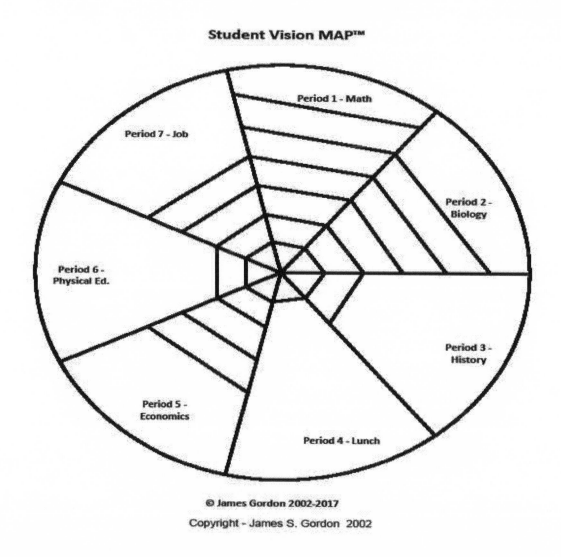

Period 1 - Math

Period 7 - Job

Period 2 - Biology

Period 6 - Physical Ed.

Period 3 - History

Period 5 - Economics

Period 4 - Lunch

© James Gordon 2002-2017
Copyright - James S. Gordon 2002

Some people think that it is peculiar to add a Vision MAP™ for a lunch period, but it doesn't take much thought or recall in terms of considering how some students chose to use this period – most students use the time constructively – yet other students need to learn how to better utilize their time. And improve their choices for nourishment.

The next VMAP is a blank version of the Student Vision MAP™, above.

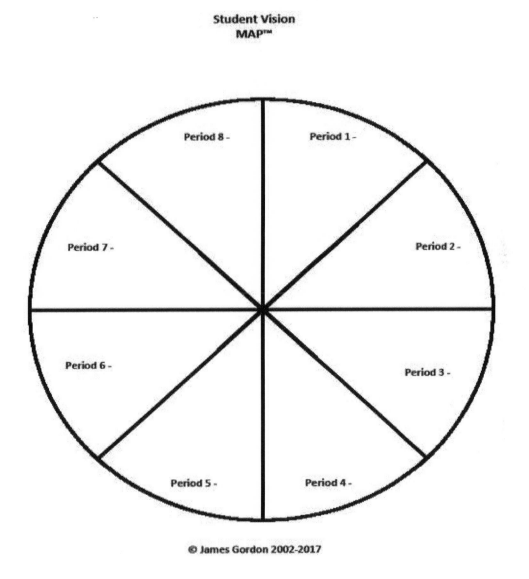

Student Vision MAP™

Period 8 -

Period 1 -

Period 7 -

Period 2 -

Period 6 -

Period 3 -

Period 5 -

Period 4 -

© James Gordon 2002-2017

Copyright - James S. Gordon 2002

Success Vision MAP™. This Vision MAP™ serves as a benchmark - a road map to the acquisition of the skills, knowledge and attitudes the district, parents and student value.

There is an opportunity for faculty, parents, and students to use the alignment tool to refine what success means to each stakeholder – should they choose to explore this option.

Success Vision MAP™

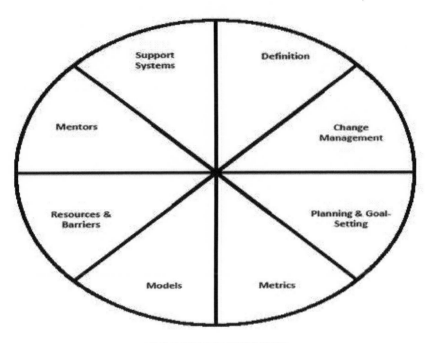

© James Gordon 2002-2017

Copyright - James S. Gordon 2002

Failure Vision MAP™. Failure analysis is a part of NASA's space flight operations. Even when there are no accidents, there are sometimes small systems' flaws, errors or failures which must be corrected or eliminated before the next flight. It is the team or organization charged with these tasks that save lives and dollars for future operations.

Learning from mistakes and failures must be taught as some people learn to generalize a failure as a way of life.

I recall asking participants in one of my workshops, if I could teach you how to fail at any thing that you attempt – how valuable would that knowledge be? The first student to reply answered "I don't want to fail at things that I attempt". A subsequent student's answer included the reference to learning what failure entails – not actually failing. If there is a known quantity called failure – would it not be worthwhile to have failure identified from the outset – perhaps to avoid it?

I believe and have advocated for a Community of Practice (CoP) formed to de-mystify and de-stigmatize failure for the benefit of all people. Learning the height, depth, and breadth of failure helps us to understand how normal and "unavoidable" it is along with how to withstand and prosper from what is referred to as failure.

Failure is currently studied via Failure Analysis, Root Cause Analysis, and Root Cause Failure Analysis. I've add to this mix the term Root Cause Human Failure Analysis.

We may not be discussing the "mean time between failures" for relationships or businesses any time soon. However, my "research" into this area over a 20+ years span has taught me that people need / deserve our thought leaders' (re: failure analysis) best efforts to help us to reap the rewards that failure can / will yield.

Failure Vision MAP™

© James Gordon 2002-2017

Copyright - James S. Gordon 2002

Exit Strategies Vision MAP™

One of the lessons learned from my years of Workforce Development training is that people oftentimes get themselves into situations or predicaments – yet they have no clear understanding as to how to extricate themselves from that situation.

Vision Mapping™ "Exit Strategies" illustrates the skills and knowledge needed for planning a transition from tasks, groups, relationships, or circumstances that are not healthy or constructive or have simply "outlived" their / its usefulness.

I recommend asking for help from someone you trust as there are times when professional advice (lawyer, therapist, etc.) is needed to get you free from an entanglement or "enmeshment".

Exit Strategies Vision MAP™

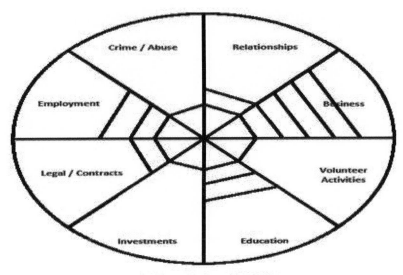

© James Gordon 2002-2017

Copyright - James S. Gordon 2002

75

Study Skills Vision MAP™

Like all of the previous Vision MAP™s, the Study Skills Vision MAP™ is blank until

the end user decides or is helped with the decision(s) regarding what the contents of the

Vision MAP™ should be.

Any thing that needs to be planned can be Vision MAPped™ whether it is the school's

responsibilities, the parent's wishes, and/or the students' needs. Vision Mapping™ will

facilitate and coordinate the efforts of each stakeholder in the education process.

Study Skills Vision MAP™

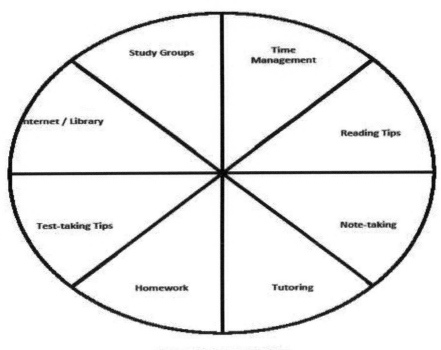

© James Gordon 2002-2017

Copyright - James S. Gordon 2002

Student Services Vision MAP™

This is an actual VMAP that I created to guide me through my doctoral program at Walden University. The date on it, i.e. January 8, 2003 represents the month that I started…

The vertical lines represented (the limits of) my understanding of the school and the services provided – along with my responsibilities on that date. That understanding grew over time. Sorry, I don't have the proverbial before and after shots for you.

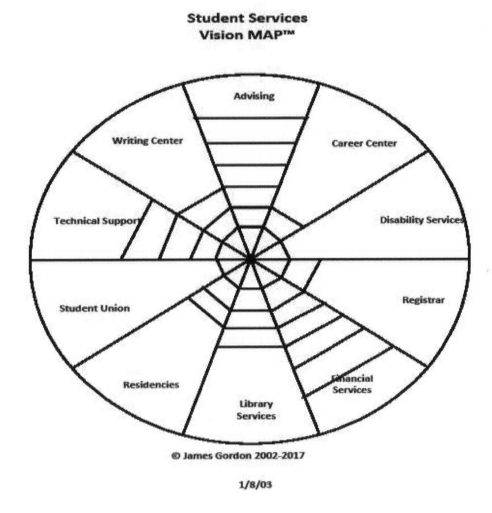

Student Services Vision MAP™

Advising

Career Center

Writing Center

Disability Services

Technical Support

Registrar

Student Union

Financial Services

Residencies

Library Services

© James Gordon 2002-2017

1/8/03

Vision Mapping™ is scalable for use at all levels of education – I've used it at home, school, and in my business. One project that I used it for was in researching strategic plans – Vision and Mission Statements to determine the extent – if any those visions and missions were evident in the position or job descriptions of the agency or business. I found little "throughput" for the vision and mission statements of large federal agencies as well as smaller state and local entities. I discussed what I found with faculty at Walden. And, I made a presentation to other students at one of my residencies – concerning this research.

A nagging question for me was why have jobs that don't reflect or incorporate the vision and / or mission of the entity wherein they are found? No one had answers (satisfactory answers).

Subsequently, I examined scores of strategic plans – published on the web sites of government, industry, schools, and local social service groups. Based on what I found in those documents, I assumed that strategic planning need a "kick in the pants" as feet needed to be placed under these documents – feet that the public and stockholders could see and understand.

This conclusion led me to expand what I am calling Vision Mapping™. I was given a business assistance grant from a national laboratory (Battelle's Pacific Northwest Lab in Richland, WA) about VMAPs (coincidentally, I once worked for another national lab – Jet Propulsion Laboratory in Pasadena, CA). My purpose is to provide an electronic version of Vision Mapping™ as its efficacy has been proven through workshops that I have conducted for hundreds of people and through my personal use of these tools.

Wrap-up

Initially, your VMAPs may be pencil and paper inventories of the things that you hold dear. Some of you will reduce your lists and drawings into an electronic format. I created over 1,500 scenarios in which one might use a VMAP. There is a good chance that all the templates that you will need are in that 1,500+ scenarios.

I may find, at some point, that I need 500 more scenarios – fleshed out. I'll look for a way to make generic VMAPs – at least the personal VMAP, the aligned VMAP, and the Meta VMAPs available to those of you who read this book.

If you share this book with others, please remember that my book on goal discovery may be a better match for them.

APPENDIX A
More VMAPs

(Writing A) Book Vision MAP™

I've dreamed of writing a book for close to 30 years. But, it was not until I created a Vision MAP™ that I saw that it was possible as I had the tools / resources to complete the book – this is my third book – I've got two more books on the drawing board for 2017 (…ghost writing this time).

Book Vision MAP™

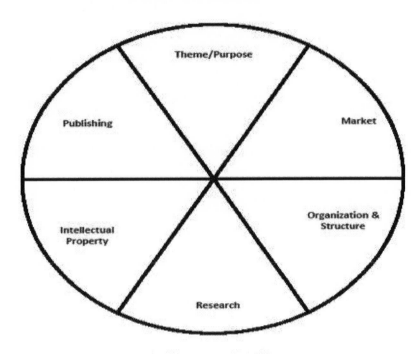

© James Gordon 2002-2017

Copyright – James S. Gordon 2002

Retirement Vision MAP™

I believe that you must be the architect of your retirement as you have been for your work life. I trust that borrowing a Haiku poem from my little booklet of poems can illustrate my thinking regarding retirement:

"Judged"

You will be judged not
by your accumulations
but by what you give

Finding a way to give to others – doesn't have to be to the "less fortunate". I've found people of means also have needs that you may be able to fill.

Some of us will choose to "retire". Please know that there is a transition phase / process in play when you retire from work. That transition to retirement needs to be understood and mapped. You now have the tools to help yourself or others make retirement rewarding and fun.

Retirement Vision MAP™

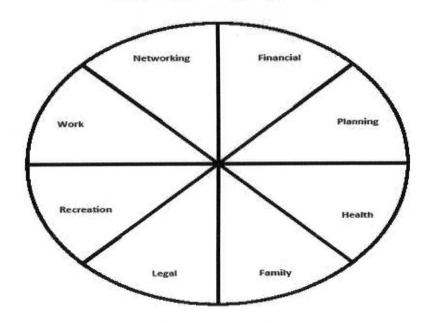

© James Gordon 2002-2017

Copyright - James S. Gordon 2002

Financial Transition Vision MAP™

Having no crystal ball, we ought to plan for financial contingencies or changes that may occur. The transition is made easier when we have a plan to ameliorate the perceived or actual damage / harm that is caused by the event(s) listed, below.

I worked for six years as a Life and Health insurance agent and a Series 7 "stockbroker". During and since that time, I've seen serious blows to families' well-being due to what I'm calling financial transition.

Financial Transition Vision MAP™

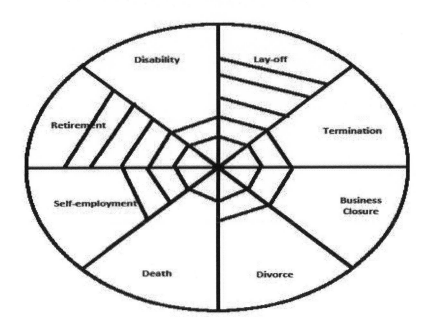

© James Gordon 2002-2017

Copyright - James S. Gordon 2002

Human Resources Vision MAP™

Straight out of the University of Wisconsin-Madison, I worked in "Personnel" (now HR) for eight years. I had the chance to see planning and goal setting, first hand. Not sure whether the enclosed snapshot is a current or original assessment of my knowledge of Human Resources.

The flexibility of Vision Mapping™ allows the user(s) to make up-to-the-minute changes – whenever they are warranted.

An electronic version of Vision Mapping™ will allow the organization the opportunity to assist with the roll out of Vision Mapping™ for the entire organization.

Human Resources Vision MAP™

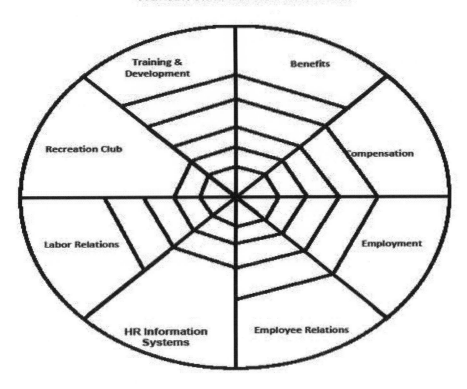

© James Gordon 2002-2017

Copyright - James S. Gordon 2002

School District Vision MAP™

I'd like to tell you that the VMAP, below, is a product of my inside knowledge of the inner workings of our local school districts, but it is not. However, I have reviewed strategic plans of local school districts – so it is not a total fiction.

We can, prospectively, VMAP a topic, place, or activity for a later "deep dive". The parents with the two year old, above, conducted research on the schools that they wanted to send their child to. We can do the same in various areas – to be prepared for that desired outcome that we VMAPped.

School Vision MAP™

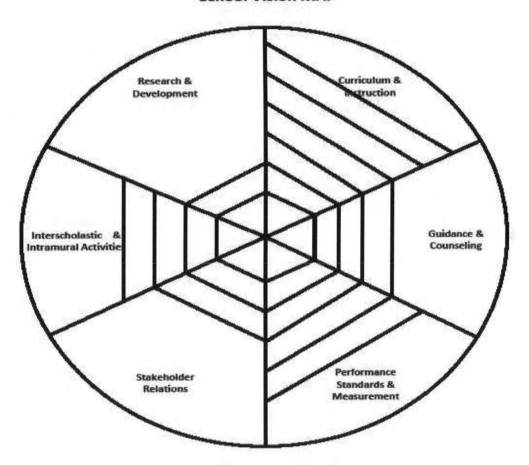

© James Gordon 2002-2017

Copyright - James S. Gordon 2002

Transferable Skills Vision MAP™

If you are looking for work or changing jobs / careers, this next tool may be helpful. This VMAP is called the Transferable Skills MAP™.

Most people are not aware of the numerous transferable skills that they possess. In my job search workshops, we covered scores of transferable skills that each participant brought to the workshop.

The experts that trained us to be trainers for unemployed and displaced workers, told us that the number of skills that the average person has is well into the hundreds. We will only include six.

Transferable Skills Vision MAP™

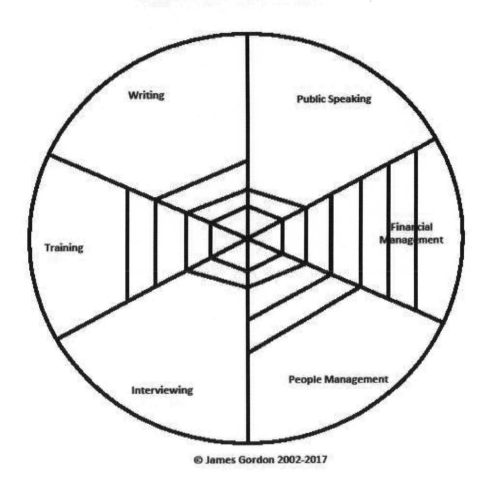

© James Gordon 2002-2017

Copyright - James S. Gordon 2002

These are skills that most people will need throughout their careers. Youth should learn these skills before high school graduation. One can use these skills to obtain a job and they will certainly need them to keep the job. Even, as an entrepreneur you will need

them – to obtain and keep customers, vendors, and employees. You can Vision MAP (used as a verb) to acquire transferable skills – there many more worthwhile skills that you may need. If you have a mentor or someone in your field that you hold in high esteem, ask for her or his thoughts on what traits and skills you will need to excel in your field.

Throughput of Visions and Missions

What follows is an example of the failure of a vision or mission to be transferred to or manifested in the end result of one or more planners. Although, this example is for an organization, it applies to a personal planning project, too.

For all the effort and expense that we put into strategic planning, there is a problem that I have heard discussed – directly. I've been in meetings wherein there was a focus on why a result or two was not accomplished. No one attributed the problem to a failure in the "integrity" of the planning system, in play.

After studying a federal agency's job description, I found that the stated vision and mission for the agency was not "apparent" in the job descriptions of the agency. Prior to this research, that agency was in the news – problems… I wondered why do the work if there was no nexus to the vision and mission of the agency.

I examined other organizations – public and private that publish their strategic plans and job descriptions, too. I found this specific problem along with a few other problems that may have their genesis in the lack of or inadequate throughput to the desired outcome of the planners.

Part of what is being called throughput are:

- Critical Success Factors

- Critical Failure Factors

- Five Common Errors***

In the book "Decision Sciences…" Kleindorfer et al state that there are three common problems found in the problem-solving process:

1. ***Type I Error: Detecting a problem when there isn't one.
2. ***Type II Error: Not detecting a problem when there is one.
3. ***Type III Error: Solving the wrong problem.

After my research along these lines, I added two other "errors":

4. ***Type IV Error: Failure to execute the solution (or decision alternative) – due to:
   - Lack of time
   - Lack of resources - money, car, tools, computer, home, etc.
   - Lack of will – fear or threats may contribute to this situation. There is the potential for (or actual) "blowback" – blowback entails real or imaged negative consequences from pursuing a given course of action

5. ***Type V Error: Problem Nesting / Clusters. Typically, these are multi-faceted or complex problems. For example, some of the social services clients that I provided job search training for faced problem clusters, e.g.

   - loss of job and a divorce…
   - substance abuse and a criminal record…
   - lack of GED and no work experience…
   - illness or disability and job obsolescence…
   - permutations of the foregoing problems…

Kleindorfer, P. R. K., Howard, C.; Schoemaker, P.J.H. (1993).
<u>Decision Sciences - An Integrative Perspective</u>. Cambridge, United Kingdom, Cambridge University Press

These errors may cause or exacerbate the "disconnect" in terms of the throughput failing to ensure the accomplishment of the desired outcome(s).

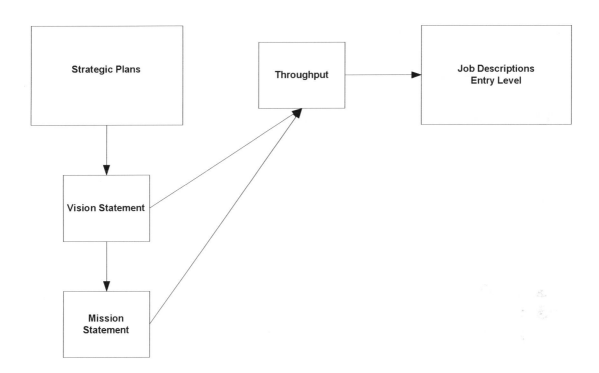

Competition Vision MAP™

This VMAP is intended to be used in business application – not the participation in sports or games. Any person wanting to go into business must be able to determine the nature and quality of the prospective and current competition.

Competition Vision MAP™

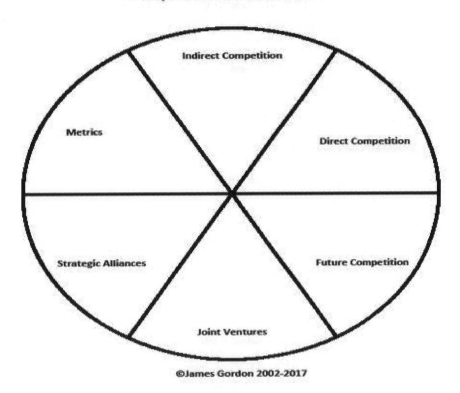

©James Gordon 2002-2017

Copyright - James S. Gordon 2002

Investment Vision MAP™

When I worked in financial services, we had a tool entitled "Financial Needs Analysis". We used it to illustrate the value of our approach to financial security using our tools and assistance. Quite slick and persuasive as we relied on the promise of "compounding" to fill the need left by the loss or disability of a loved one.

Just as we started with a glossary in this book, financial services representative would do well to educate their clients on the basics – contained in the VMAP, above. Otherwise, as customers we end up dropping or switching plans with the next slick presentation.

Investment Vision MAP™

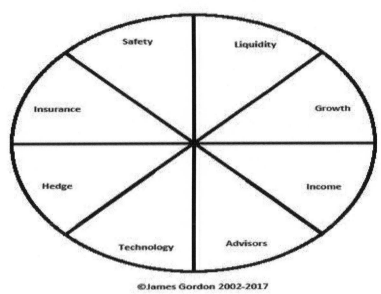

©James Gordon 2002-2017

Copyright - James S. Gordon 2002

Appendix B – Reference Book Definitions for Vision Continuum™ Terms

The American Heritage® Dictionary of the English Language, Fourth Edition. Copyright © 2000 by Houghton Mifflin Company. Published by the Houghton Mifflin Company. All rights reserved. © 1996-2002 yourDictionary.com, Inc. All Rights Reserved.

ob·jec·tive
(click to hear the word) (b-j k t v)
adj.
1. Of or having to do with a material object.
2. Having actual existence or reality.
3.
a. Uninfluenced by emotions or personal prejudices: *an objective critic.*
See Synonyms at fair1.
b. Based on observable phenomena; presented factually: *an objective appraisal.*
4. *Medicine* Indicating a symptom or condition perceived as a sign of disease by someone other than the person affected.
5. *Grammar*
a. Of, relating to, or being the case of a noun or pronoun that serves as

goal
(click to hear the word) (g l)
n.
1. The purpose toward which an endeavor is directed; an objective. See Synonyms at intention.
2. *Sports*
a. The finish line of a race.
b. A specified structure or zone into or over which players endeavor to advance a ball or puck.
c. The score awarded for such an act.
3. *Linguistics*
a. A noun or noun phrase referring to the place to which something moves.
b. See patient.
[Middle English gol, *boundary*, possibly from Old English *g l, *barrier.*]
the object of a verb.
b. Of or relating to a noun or pronoun used in this case.
n.
1. Something that actually exists.
2. Something worked toward or striven for; a goal. See Synonyms at intention.
3. *Grammar*
a. The objective case.

b. A noun or pronoun in the objective case.

4. The lens or lens system in a microscope or other optical instrument that first receives light rays from the object and forms the image. Also called *object glass*, *objective lens*, *object lens*.

ob·jec tive·ly *adv.*

ob·jec tive·ness *n.*

The American Heritage® Dictionary of the English Language, Fourth Edition. Copyright © 2000 by Houghton Mifflin Company. Published by
the Houghton Mifflin Company. All rights reserved.
© 1996-2002 yourDictionary.com, Inc. All Rights Reserved.

vi·sion

(click to hear the word) (v zh n)

n.

1.

a. The faculty of sight; eyesight: *poor vision.*

b. Something that is or has been seen.

2. Unusual competence in discernment or perception; intelligent foresight: *a leader of vision.*

3. The manner in which one sees or conceives of something.

4. A mental image produced by the imagination.

5. The mystical experience of seeing as if with the eyes the supernatural or a supernatural being.

6. A person or thing of extraordinary beauty.

tr.v. **vi·sioned**, **vi·sion·ing**, **vi·sions**

To see in or as if in a vision; envision.

[Middle English, from Old French, from Latin v si , v si n-, from v sus, past participle of vid re, *to see*; see weid- in Indo-European roots.]

vi sion·al *adj.*

vi sion·al·ly *adv.*

The American Heritage® Dictionary of the English Language, Fourth Edition. Copyright © 2000 by Houghton Mifflin Company. Published by
the Houghton Mifflin Company. All rights reserved.
© 1996-2002 yourDictionary.com, Inc. All Rights Reserved.

mis·sion

(click to hear the word) (m sh n)

n.

1.

a. A body of persons sent to conduct negotiations or establish relations with a foreign country.

b. The business with which such a body of persons is charged.

c. A permanent diplomatic office abroad.

d. A body of experts or dignitaries sent to a foreign country.

2.

a. A body of persons sent to a foreign land by a religious organization,

especially a Christian organization, to spread its faith or provide
educational, medical, and other assistance.
b. A mission established abroad.
c. The district assigned to a mission worker.
d. A building or compound housing a mission.
e. An organization for carrying on missionary work in a territory.
f. **missions** Missionary duty or work.
3. A Christian church or congregation with no cleric of its own that depends for
support on a larger religious organization.
4. A series of special Christian services for purposes of proselytizing.
5. A welfare or educational organization established for the needy people of a
district.
6.
a. A special assignment given to a person or group: *an agent on a secret
mission.*
b. A combat operation assigned to a person or military unit.
c. An aerospace operation intended to carry out specific program
objectives: *a mission to Mars.*
7. An inner calling to pursue an activity or perform a service; a vocation.
tr.v. **mis·sioned**, **mis·sion·ing**, **mis·sions**
1. To send on a mission.
2. To organize or establish a religious mission among or in.
adj.
1. Of or relating to a mission.
2. Of or relating to a style of architecture or furniture used in the early Spanish
missions of California.
3. often **Mission** Of, relating to, or having the distinctive qualities of an early
20th-century style of plain, heavy, dark-stained wood furniture.
[French, from Old French, from Latin missi , missi n-, from missus, past participle
of mittere, *to send off.*]
mis sion·al *adj.*

The American Heritage® Dictionary of the English Language, Fourth Edition. Copyright © 2000 by Houghton
Mifflin Company. Published by
the Houghton Mifflin Company. All rights reserved.
© 1996-2002 yourDictionary.com, Inc. All Rights Reserved.

plan
(click to hear the word) (pl n)
n.
1. A scheme, program, or method worked out beforehand for the
accomplishment of an objective: *a plan of attack.*
2. A proposed or tentative project or course of action: *had no plans for the
evening.*
3. A systematic arrangement of elements or important parts; a configuration or
outline: *a seating plan; the plan of a story.*
4. A drawing or diagram made to scale showing the structure or arrangement of
something.

5. In perspective rendering, one of several imaginary planes perpendicular to the line of vision between the viewer and the object being depicted.

6. A program or policy stipulating a service or benefit: *a pension plan.*

***v.* planned, plan·ning, plans**

v. tr.

1. To formulate a scheme or program for the accomplishment, enactment, or attainment of: *plan a campaign.*

2. To have as a specific aim or purpose; intend: *They plan to buy a house.*

3. To draw or make a graphic representation of.

v. intr.

To make plans.

[French, alteration (influenced by plan, *flat surface*), of plant, *ground plan, map* from planter, *to plant*, from Latin plant re, from planta, *sole of the foot*; see plat- in Indo-European roots.]

plan ner *n.*

Synonyms: *plan, blueprint, design, project, scheme, strategy*

These nouns denote a method or program in accordance with which something is to be done or accomplished: *has no vacation plans; a blueprint for reorganizing the company; social conventions of human design; an urban-renewal project; a new scheme for conservation; a strategy for survival.*

The American Heritage® Dictionary of the English Language, Fourth Edition. Copyright © 2000 by Houghton Mifflin Company. Published by the Houghton Mifflin Company. All rights reserved. © 1996-2002 yourDictionary.com, Inc. All Rights Reserved.

task

(click to hear the word) (t sk)

n.

1. A piece of work assigned or done as part of one's duties.

2. A difficult or tedious undertaking.

3. A function to be performed; an objective.

tr.v. **tasked, task·ing, tasks**

1. To assign a task to or impose a task on.

2. To overburden with labor; tax.

Idiom:

take/call/bring to task

To reprimand or censure.

[Middle English taske, *imposed work, tax*, from Old North French tasque, from Vulgar Latin *tasca, alteration of *taxa, from Latin tax re, *to feel, reproach, reckon* ; see **tax.**]

Synonyms: *task, job*1, *chore, stint*1, *assignment*

These nouns denote a piece of work that one must do. A *task* is a welldefined responsibility that is usually imposed by another and that may be burdensome: *I stayed at work late to finish the task at hand. Job* often suggests a specific short-term undertaking: *"did little jobs about the house with skill" (W.H. Auden). Chore* generally denotes a minor, routine, or odd job: *The farmer's morning chores included milking the cows. Stint* refers to a person's prescribed share of work: *Her stint as a lifeguard usually consumes three hours a day. Assignment* generally denotes a task allotted by a person in authority: *His homework assignment involved writing an essay.*

The American Heritage® Dictionary of the English Language, Fourth Edition. Copyright © 2000 by Houghton Mifflin Company. Published by the Houghton Mifflin Company. All rights reserved.
© 1996-2002 yourDictionary.com, Inc. All Rights Reserved.

Infoplease.com

vi•sion

Pronunciation: (vizh'*u*n), [key]
—*n.*
1. the act or power of sensing with the eyes; sight.
2. the act or power of anticipating that which will or may come to be: *prophetic vision; the vision of an entrepreneur.*
3. an experience in which a personage, thing, or event appears vividly or credibly to the mind, although not actually present, often under the influence of a divine or other agency: *a heavenly messenger appearing in a vision.* Cf. **hallucination** (def. 1).
4. something seen or otherwise perceived during such an experience: *The vision revealed its message.*
5. a vivid, imaginative conception or anticipation: *visions of wealth and glory.*
6. something seen; an object of sight.
7. a scene, person, etc., of extraordinary beauty: *The sky was a vision of red and pink.*
8. See **computer vision.**
—*v.t.*
to envision: *She tried to vision herself in a past century.*

mis•sion

Pronunciation: (mish'*u*n), [key]
—*n.*
1. a group or committee of persons sent to a foreign country to conduct negotiations, establish relations, provide scientific and technical assistance, or the like.
2. the business with which such a group is charged.
3. a permanent diplomatic establishment abroad; embassy; legation.
4. *Mil.*an operational task, usually assigned by a higher headquarters: *a mission to bomb the bridge.*
5. *Aerospace.*an operation designed to carry out the goals of a specific program: *a space mission.*
6. a group of persons sent by a church to carry on religious work, esp. evangelization in foreign lands, and often to establish schools, hospitals, etc.
7. an establishment of missionaries in a foreign land; a missionary church or station.
8. a similar establishment in any region.
9. the district assigned to a missionary.
10. missionary duty or work.
11. an organization for carrying on missionary work.
12. Also called **rescue mission.** a shelter operated by a church or other organization offering food, lodging, and other assistance to needy persons.
13. missions, organized missionary work or activities in any country or region.
14. a church or a region dependent on a larger church or denomination.
15. a series of special religious services for increasing religious devotion and converting unbelievers: *to preach a mission.*

16. an assigned or self-imposed duty or task; calling; vocation.

17. a sending or being sent for some duty or purpose.

18. those sent.

—*adj.*

1. of or pertaining to a mission.

2. (*usually cap.*) noting or pertaining to a style of American furniture of the early 20th century, created in supposed imitation of the furnishings of the Spanish missions of California and characterized by the use of dark, stained wood, by heaviness, and by extreme plainness. Also called **foreign mission** (for defs. 3, 6).

Mis•sion

plan

Pronunciation: (plan), [key]

—*n., v.,* planned, plan•ning.

—*n.*

1. a scheme or method of acting, doing, proceeding, making, etc., developed in advance: *battle plans.*

2. a design or scheme of arrangement: *an elaborate plan for seating guests.*

3. a specific project or definite purpose: *plans for the future.*

4. Also called **plan view.** a drawing made to scale to represent the top view or a horizontal section of a structure or a machine, as a floor layout of a building.

5. a representation of a thing drawn on a plane, as a map or diagram: *a plan of the dock area.*

6. (in perspective drawing) one of several planes in front of a represented object, and perpendicular to the line between the object and the eye.

7. a formal program for specified benefits, needs, etc.: *a pension plan.*

—*v.t.*

1. to arrange a method or scheme beforehand for (any work, enterprise, or proceeding): *to plan a new recreation center.*

2. to make plans for: *to plan one's vacation.*

3. to draw or make a diagram or layout of, as a building.

—*v.i.*

to make plans: *to plan ahead; to plan for one's retirement.*

plan-

goal

Pronunciation: (gOl), [key]

—*n.*

1. the result or achievement toward which effort is directed; aim; end.

2. the terminal point in a race.

3. a pole, line, or other marker by which such a point is indicated.

4. an area, basket, cage, or other object or structure toward or into which players of various games attempt to throw, carry, kick, hit, or drive a ball, puck, etc., to score a point or points.

5. the act of throwing, carrying, kicking, driving, etc., a ball or puck into such an area or object.

6. the score made by this act.

ob•jec•tive

Pronunciation: (*u*b-jek'tiv), [key]

—*n.*

1. something that one's efforts or actions are intended to attain or accomplish; purpose; goal;

target: *the objective of a military attack; the objective of a fund-raising drive.*

2. *Gram.*

a. Also called **objective case.** (in English and some other languages) a case specialized for the use of a form as the object of a transitive verb or of a preposition, as *him* in *The boy hit him,* or *me* in *He comes to me with his troubles.*

b. a word in that case.

3. Also called **object glass, object lens, objective lens.** *Optics.*(in a telescope, microscope, camera, or other optical system) the lens or combination of lenses that first receives the rays from the object and forms the image in the focal plane of the eyepiece, as in a microscope, or on a plate or screen, as in a camera. See diag. under **microscope.**

—*adj.*

1. being the object or goal of one's efforts or actions.

2. not influenced by personal feelings, interpretations, or prejudice; based on facts; unbiased: *an objective opinion.*

3. intent upon or dealing with things external to the mind rather than with thoughts or feelings, as a person or a book.

4. being the object of perception or thought; belonging to the object of thought rather than to the thinking subject (opposed to *subjective*).

5. of or pertaining to something that can be known, or to something that is an object or a part of an object; existing independent of thought or an observer as part of reality.

6. *Gram.*

a. pertaining to the use of a form as the object of a transitive verb or of a preposition.

b. (in English and some other languages) noting the objective case.

c. similar to such a case in meaning.

d. (in case grammar) pertaining to the semantic role of a noun phrase that denotes something undergoing a change of state or bearing a neutral relation to the verb, as *the rock* in *The rock moved* or in *The child threw the rock.*

7. being part of or pertaining to an object to be drawn: *an objective plane.*

8. *Med.*(of a symptom) discernible to others as well as the patient.

task

Pronunciation: (task, täsk), [key]

—*n.*

1. a definite piece of work assigned to, falling to, or expected of a person; duty.

2. any piece of work.

3. a matter of considerable labor or difficulty.

4. *Obs.*a tax or impost.

5. take to task, to call to account; blame; censure: *The teacher took them to task for not doing their homework.*

—*v.t.*

1. to subject to severe or excessive labor or exertion; put a strain upon (powers, resources, etc.).

2. to impose a task on.

3. *Obs.*to tax.

—*adj*
.

of or pertaining to a task or tasks: *A task chart will help organize the department's work.*
Visine visional

goal
(click to hear the word) (gōl)

n.

1. The purpose toward which an endeavor is directed; an objective. See Synonyms at intention.
2. *Sports*
    a. The finish line of a race.
    b. A specified structure or zone into or over which players endeavor to advance a ball or puck.
    c. The score awarded for such an act.
3. *Linguistics*
    a. A noun or noun phrase referring to the place to which something moves.
    b. See patient.

[Middle English gol, *boundary*, possibly from Old English *gāl, *barrier*.]

⌃ BACK TO TOP

The American Heritage® Dictionary of the English Language, Fourth Edition. Copyright © 2000 by Houghton Mifflin Company. Published by the Houghton Mifflin Company. All rights reserved.

© 1996-2002 yourDictionary.com, Inc. All Rights Reserved.

ob·jec·tive
(click to hear the word) (əb-jĕk'tĭv)

adj.

1. Of or having to do with a material object.
2. Having actual existence or reality.
3.
    a. Uninfluenced by emotions or personal prejudices: *an objective critic.* See Synonyms at fair[1].
    b. Based on observable phenomena; presented factually: *an objective appraisal.*
4. *Medicine* Indicating a symptom or condition perceived as a sign of disease by someone other than the person affected.
5. *Grammar*
    a. Of, relating to, or being the case of a noun or pronoun that serves as

Made in the USA
Las Vegas, NV
14 January 2021

15890629R10065